The Writer's Book  of Inspiration

Dear Revel,

It is an honor to include your work.

Love,

Also by Stephanie Gunning:

The Writer's
Book *of*
Inspiration

Quotes on Writing
and the Literary Life

Selected and edited by

Stephanie Gunning

Creative Blast Press
New York, NY

Creative Blast Press is a division of Stephanie Gunning Enterprises LLC. Creative Blast Press books are available at quantity discounts for educational, business, or sales promotional use. For information, please email: contact@stephaniegunning.com.

Cover and interior design by Gus Yoo

978-0-9849926-2-1 (paperback)

978-0-9849926-3-8 (ebook)

1. Quotations 2. Motivation 3. Inspiration 4. Creativity 5. Writing 6. Authorship 7. Self-help

To those who dare write

Contents

Preface

Writing is love. It's the beating heart pulsing on paper. It is music, magic, and mystery, an effort to gain mastery of forces, of impulses, of desires, of ideas, of life. To those who feel an intense magnetic pull to write, little explanation of the phenomenon is required. You know who you are. You also know the pull is only the beginning. There is a reason others look upon those who write as they would mythical creatures, like unicorns and dragons: Writers have the power to name and to reveal. Once you sense this possibility in yourself, you likely will be hooked on it forever.

Yes, writers are admired. But writers should also be suspect. Watch out. Everything is fair game to writers. Their lives, meaning literally anything and everything they feel, think, do, experience, observe, or dream about, can, and probably will, show up in their poems, plays, films, essays, and books. As admirable as they may be, writers can also be dangerous.

As a writer myself, I feel I'm always trying to capture fireflies in a jar. But how does one capture a dynamic, moving force like life or an emotion in images without it losing its vitality? How can one put a frame around a picture that has no beginning and no end? I always do my best to approximate my perceptions in words. But some days I'm a better writer than on other days. Some days my writing sucks. On the best days, there's nothing like the feeling of writing.

No one can stop you from writing if you want to write. That's one of the beautiful things about it. You might think that someone else has to give you permission. That's a false belief. Writers really get better at writing when they stop looking for approval—both their own and others'. For encouragement, I used to keep a note stuck up above my desk that read: "Be bold." Then there was the time in a Chinese restaurant that I got a fortune cookie informing me, "One day you will write a book." I taped that above my computer screen. Whatever message you need to hear to grant yourself the freedom to write whatever you want to write, tell it to yourself.

It's only human nature to compare ourselves to other people and study their habits. It's human to want to belong to a tribe, to fit in. For these reasons, it is fun to observe how other writers write and live. *How do they do it? What does it mean to them? Am I the same way?* I hope you'll be excited to flip around in this book and see what random pages you land on.

When I began compiling the quotations for this book I was impressed with the extraordinary highs and lows creative writers experience while pursuing the craft. Some describe virtually tearing their hair out in desperation, others are pragmatic, even mercenary, and compulsive, and many express delight and spiritual wonder. The ones I love best are those that provoked me to laugh and to think. They all made me proud to call myself a writer and lifted my self-esteem. In these remarks from men and women of different ages, races, and eras, I felt a mirror being held up to my daily life as a craftsperson, an artist, and a living human being. There is a tremendous humanity to be found in how they go about, and often struggle at, doing their best work. Nothing else matters more, when you get right down to it, than being human—with all that it means.

The literary life is a path of self-discovery and revelation. If you have chosen to walk this well-worn path, remember to step a little bit outside of the bounds of cultural expectations from time to time. Trample the grass—or better, take off your shoes and feel the grass between your toes. Never rush and always daydream. Nap at strange hours. Design your own rituals. Ignore the ringing telephone, and other forms of buzzing, chiming, beeping technology. Let yourself forget what day of the week it is. Travel. Read. Cultivate relationships with odd and curious people. Whatever it is you feel, whatever you think or believe, make the blank page your friend and no matter where you go you'll be at home and have something to do. Be surprised by life.

Stephanie Gunning
January 2013
New York City

On
Writing
and the

Literary
Life

"O for a Muse of fire, that would ascend The brightest heaven of invention . . ."

— WILLIAM SHAKESPEARE

"We write to taste life twice, in the moment and in retrospection."

— A N A Ï S   N I N

"Writing is a habit, an addiction, as powerful and overmastering an urge as putting a bottle to your lips or a spike in your arm. Call it the impulse to make something out of nothing, call it an obsessive-compulsive disorder, call it logorrhea."

— T . C . B O Y L E

"There are three rules for writing a novel. Unfortunately, no one knows what they are."

— W. Somerset Maugham

"The only way you can write the truth is to assume that what you set down will never be read. Not by any other person, and not even by yourself at some later date. Otherwise you begin excusing yourself. You must see the writing as emerging like a long scroll of ink from the index finger of your right hand; you must see your left hand erasing it."

—MARGARET ATWOOD

"They're fancy talkers about themselves, writers. If I had to give young writers advice, I would say don't listen to writers talk about writing or themselves."

—LILLIAN HELLMAN

"Creativity is allowing yourself to make mistakes. Art is knowing which ones to keep."

—SCOTT ADAMS

"I never exactly made a book.

It's rather like taking dictation.

I was given things to say."

— C . S .   L E W I S

"If the artist does not fling himself, without reflecting, into his work, as Curtis flung himself into the yawning gulf, as the soldier flings himself into the enemy's trenches, and if, once in this crater, he does not work like a miner on whom the walls of his gallery have fallen in; if he contemplates difficulties instead of overcoming them one by one . . . he is simply looking on at the suicide of his own talent."

— HONORÉ DE BALZAC

"There are no mistakes. What happens during the process of making something is sacred and organic."

—Vicki Noble

"That's the essential goal of the writer: you slice out a piece of yourself and slap it down on the desk in front of you.

You try to put it on paper, try to describe it in a way that the reader can see and feel and touch. You paste all your nerve endings into it and then give it out to strangers who don't know you or understand you."

— STEPHEN LEIGH

"Writing is a job, a talent, but it's also the place to go in your head. It is the imaginary friend you drink your tea with in the afternoon."

—A N N   P A T C H E T T

"The spirit of creation is the spirit of contradiction. It is the breakthrough of appearances toward an unknown reality."

—JEAN COCTEAU

"The best time for planning a book is while you're doing the dishes."

—AGATHA CHRISTIE

"Ideas are like rabbits. You get a couple and learn how to handle them, and pretty soon you have a dozen."

—John Steinbeck

"You must stay drunk on writing so reality cannot destroy you."

— R AY   B RADBURY

"Writing is both mask and unveiling."

— E. B. WHITE

"You can't blame a writer for what the characters say."

— TRUMAN CAPOTE

"Read, read, read. Read everything—trash, classics, good and bad, and see how they do it. Just like a carpenter who works as an apprentice and studies the master. Read! You'll absorb it. Then write. If it's good, you'll find out. If it's not, throw it out of the window."

—William Faulkner

"A room without books is like a body without a soul."

— MARCUS TULLIUS CICERO

"What really knocks me out is a book that, when you're all done reading it, you wish the author that wrote it was a terrific friend of yours and you could call him up on the phone whenever you felt like it."

— J. D. SALINGER

"No one says a novel has to be one thing.

It can be anything it wants to be,

a vaudeville show, the six o'clock news,

the mumblings of wild men saddled

by demons."

—Ishmael Reed

"Until I was about seven, I thought books were just there, like trees. When I learned that people actually wrote them, I wanted to, too, because all children aspire to inhuman feats like flying. Most people grow up to realize they can't fly. Writers are people who don't grow up to realize they can't be God."

— FRAN LEBOWITZ

"Outside of a dog, a book is man's best friend. Inside of a dog it's too dark to read."

— GROUCHO MARX

"That you can learn to write better is one of our fundamental assumptions. No sensible person would deny the mystery of talent, or for that matter the mystery of inspiration. But if it is vain to deny these mysteries, it is useless to depend on them. No other art form is so infinitely mutable. Writing is revision. All prose responds to work"

— TRACY KIDDER

"The reason that fiction is more interesting than any other form of literature, to those who really like to study people, is that in fiction the author can really tell the truth without humiliating himself."

— ELEANOR ROOSEVELT

"I love deadlines. I love the whooshing noise they make as they go by."

— DOUGLAS ADAMS

"The creative mind doesn't require logical transitions from one thought to another. It skips, jumps, doubles back, circles, and dives from one idea to the next."

— B O N N I   G O L D B E R G

"There is no greater agony than bearing an untold story inside you."

— MAYA ANGELOU

"Writing a book is an adventure. To begin with it is a toy and amusement. Then it becomes a mistress, then it becomes a master, then it becomes a tyrant. The last phase is that just as you are about to be reconciled to your servitude, you kill the monster and fling him out to the public."

—WINSTON CHURCHILL

"Some editors are failed writers, but so are most writers."

— T . S . E l i o t

"*Success comes to a writer, as a rule, so gradually that it is always something of a shock to him to look back and realize the heights to which he has climbed.*"

— P. G. WODEHOUSE

"Only those things are beautiful which are inspired by madness and written by reason."

—ANDRÉ GIDE

"I have always had more dread of a pen, a bottle of ink, and a sheet of paper than of a sword or pistol."

—ALEXANDRE DUMAS

"Writer's block is only a failure of the ego."

—NORMAN MAILER

"Somewhere long ago I heard someone say that the physical act of continuous motion of your pen on paper connects your brain to your heart through your fingertips. You plug in your intuition. So, I write by hand every day. I doodle. I keep lists of ideas, which become a crazy haiku that I can sometimes decipher."

—SUZI BAUM

"There is something delicious about writing the first words of a story. You never quite know where they'll take you."

— B E A T R I X   P O T T E R

"To write well, express yourself like the common people, but think like a wise man."

— A R I S T O T L E

"I like to write when I feel spiteful.
It is like having a good sneeze."

— D . H . L A W R E N C E

"If you can't annoy somebody, there is little point in writing."

— KINGSLEY AMIS

"If you think good work is somehow synonymous with perfect work, you are headed for big trouble. Art is human; error is human; ergo art is error."

—DAVID BAYLES AND TED ORLAND

"Writing is like sex. First you do it for love, then you do it for your friends, and then you do it for money."

— VIRGINIA WOOLF

"The artist is a receptacle for emotions that come from all over the place; from the sky, from the earth, from a scrap of paper, from a passing shape, from a spider's web."

— PABLO PICASSO

*"Writers need anchoring rituals. Mine?
I've got to start with a clean desk in the
morning, unplug the phone, wash the
dishes in the sink, and drip a mug of
strong coffee or tea before I can face my
computer. Even if I don't drink coffee,
I like having that mug near at hand.
I like making coffee or tea, because
I know it means I'm about to get down
to business."*

—STEPHANIE GUNNING

"Writing my blog is a gradual deepening for me, consisting of three phases or layers. The only way I can begin is by giving myself permission to initially just data dump stream-of-consciousness thoughts. Sometimes my first written words are: 'I don't know what to write.'"

—MERIDETH MEHLBERG

"The most essential gift for a good writer is a built-in, shockproof shit detector. This is the writer's radar."

— ERNEST HEMINGWAY

"Write the kind of story you would like to read. People will give you all sorts of advice about writing, but if you are not writing something you like, no one else will like it either."

— MEG CABOT

"What I have learned—the hard and painful way—is that I cannot wait to be in the mood to write. Instead, I must write in order to create the mood. When I write regularly, according to a set schedule, the magic takes care of itself. When I wait for The Mood and come up with every excuse in the book for why I am not writing, a whole lot of nothing happens. So, I write."

—ALLISON NAZARIAN

"You know you're a writer if you can't not write. Avoiding it makes you a miserable monster. The only thing that sets you straight is to get what's within you out and onto the page."

— FAITH FREED

"If you're going to be a writer, the first essential is just to write. Do not wait for an idea. Start writing something and the ideas will come. You have to turn the faucet on before the water starts to flow."

—L OUIS L'A MOUR

"Get it down. Take chances.
It may be bad, but it's the only way you
can do anything really good."

— WILLIAM FAULKNER

"Write while the heat is in you.
The writer who postpones the recording
of his thoughts uses an iron which has
cooled to burn a hole with. He cannot
inflame the minds of his audience."

— HENRY DAVID THOREAU

"*The most solid advice . . . for a writer is this, I think: Try to learn to breathe deeply, really to taste food when you eat, and when you sleep, really to sleep. Try as much as possible to be wholly alive, with all your might, and when you laugh, laugh like hell, and when you get angry, get good and angry. Try to be alive. You will be dead soon enough.*"

—WILLIAM SAROYAN

"Fiction is about what it is to be a human being."

—David Foster Wallace

"Write what disturbs you, what you fear, what you have not been willing to speak about. Be willing to be split open."

—NATALIE GOLDBERG

"Stop working while you still feel enthusiastic about your writing. It makes it easier to return to it later. Then turn off your thoughts as much as you can. I like to look at the natural world, walk the dog, pet the cat, and even do the dishes—all things that remind me inspiration comes from my heart, hands, and body as well as my mind."

— MARLISE WABUN WIND

"Character is the very life of fiction. Setting exists so that the character has someplace to stand. Plot exists so the character can discover what he is really like, forcing the character to choice and action. And theme exists only to make the character stand up and be somebody."

—JOHN GARDNER

"Structure is the key to narrative. These are the crucial questions any storyteller must answer: Where does it begin? Where does the beginning start to end and the middle begin? Where does the middle start to end and the end begin?"

—NORA EPHRON

"I am of the firm belief that everybody could write books and I never understand why they don't. After all, everyone speaks. Once the grammar has been learnt it is simply talking on paper and in time learning what not to say."

— BERYL BAINBRIDGE

"The person, be it gentleman or lady, who has not pleasure in a good novel, must be intolerably stupid."

—JANE AUSTEN

"Success is a finished book, a stack of pages each of which is filled with words. If you reach that point, you have won a victory over yourself no less impressive than sailing single-handed around the world."

—Tom Clancy

"The physical act of setting it down on a page doesn't take so long, but the growth of a book takes time, and most of it happens out of sight like a kind of dream work."

— KATHERINE PATERSON

"A professional writer is an amateur who didn't quit."

— RICHARD BACH

"Artists don't talk about art. Artists talk about work. If I have anything to say to young writers, it's stop thinking of writing as art. Think of it as work."

— PADDY CHAYEFSKY

"Develop an interest in life as you see it; the people, things, literature, music—the world is so rich, simply throbbing with rich treasures, beautiful souls, and interesting people. Forget yourself."

—Henry Miller

"Nothing is more satisfying than to write a good sentence. It is no fun to write lumpishly, dully, in prose the reader must plod through like wet sand. But it is a pleasure to achieve, if one can, a clear running prose that is simple yet full of surprises. This does not just happen. It requires skill, hard work, a good ear, and continued practice."

— B A R B A R A   T U C H M A N

"The great enemy of clear language is insincerity. When there is a gap between one's real and one's declared aims, one turns as it were instinctively to long words and exhausted idioms, like a cuttlefish spurting out ink."

— GEORGE ORWELL

"Here is a lesson in creative writing. First rule: Do not use semicolons. They are transvestite hermaphrodites representing absolutely nothing. All they do is show you've been to college."

— KURT VONNEGUT

"Substitute 'damn' every time you're inclined to write 'very'; your editor will delete it and the writing will be just as it should be."

— MARK TWAIN

"Cut out all these exclamation points. An exclamation point is like laughing at your own joke."

—F. SCOTT FITZGERALD

"The road to hell is paved with adverbs."

— STEPHEN KING

"My attitude toward punctuation is that it ought to be as conventional as possible. The game of golf would lose a good deal if croquet mallets and billiard cues were allowed on the putting green. You ought to be able to show that you can do it a good deal better than anyone else with the regular tools before you have a license to bring in your own improvements."

— ERNEST HEMINGWAY

"If you have any young friends who aspire to become writers, the second greatest favor you can do them is to present them with copies of The Elements of Style. *The first greatest, of course, is to shoot them now, while they're happy."*

—DOROTHY PARKER

"The writer has to take the most used, most familiar objects—nouns, pronouns, verbs, adverbs—ball them together and make them bounce, turn them a certain way and make people get into a romantic mood; and another way, into a bellicose mood. I'm most happy to be a writer."

— MAYA ANGELOU

"All good books will eventually find a publisher if the writer tries hard enough, and a central secret to writing a good book is to write on that which people like you will enjoy. Write what you care about and understand."

— RICHARD NORTH PATTERSON

"If you want to write, you can. Fear stops most people from writing, not lack of talent, whatever that is. Who am I? What right have I to speak? Who will listen to me if I do? You're a human being, with a unique story to tell, and you have every right. If you speak with passion, many of us will listen. We need stories to live, all of us. We live by story. Yours enlarges the circle."

—RICHARD RHODES

"To believe your own thought, to believe that what is true for you in your private heart is true for all men—that is genius."

—RALPH WALDO EMERSON

"The goods that a writer produces can never be impersonal; his character gets into them as certainly as it gets into the work of any other creative artist, and he must be prepared to endure investigation of it, and speculation upon it, and even gossip about it."

— H. L. MENCKEN

"*Most critical writing is drivel and half of it is dishonest. It is a shortcut to oblivion, anyway. Thinking in terms of ideas destroys the power to think in terms of emotions and sensations.*"

— RAYMOND CHANDLER

"Occasionally, there arises a writing situation where you see an alternative to what you are doing, a mad, wild gamble of a way for handling something, which may leave you looking stupid, ridiculous, or brilliant—you just don't know which. You can play it safe there, too, and proceed along the route you'd mapped out for yourself. Or you can trust your personal demon who delivered that crazy idea in the first place. Trust your demon."

—ROGER ZELAZNY

"An artist is someone who can hold two opposing viewpoints and still remain fully functional."

— F. Scott Fitzgerald

"If the doctor told me I had six minutes to live, I'd type a little faster."

—Isaac Asimov

"Work and play are the same. When you're following your energy and doing what you want all the time, the distinction between work and play dissolves."

—SHAKTI GAWAIN

"We know that attention acts as a lightning rod. Merely by concentrating on something one causes endless analogies to collect around it, even penetrate the boundaries of the subject itself: an experience that we call coincidence, serendipity—the terminology is extensive. My experience has been that in these circular travels what is really significant surrounds a central absence, an absence that, paradoxically, is the text being written or to be written."

—Julio Cortázar

"You must write every single day of your life ... You must lurk in libraries and climb the stacks like ladders to sniff books like perfumes and wear books like hats upon your crazy heads ... may you be in love every day for the next 20,000 days. And out of that love, remake a world."

— RAY BRADBURY

"If there's a book that you want to read, but it hasn't been written yet, then you must write it."

—T O N I   M O R R I S O N

*"A poet is a man who manages,
in a lifetime of standing out in
thunderstorms, to be struck by lightning
five or six times."*

— RANDALL JARRELL

"Everywhere I go, I find a poet has been there before me."

—Sigmund Freud

"I was supposed to write a romantic comedy, but my characters broke up."

— A N N B R A S H A R E S

"Writers will happen in the best of families."

—RITA MAE BROWN

"Nothing quite has reality for me till I write it all down—revising and embellishing as I go. I'm always waiting for things to be over so I can get home and commit them to paper."

—ERICA JONG

"A scrupulous writer, in every sentence that he writes, will ask himself at least four questions, thus: 1. What am I trying to say? 2. What words will express it? 3. What image or idiom will make it clearer? 4. Is this image fresh enough to have an effect?"

— George Orwell

"When I write I am trying to express my way of being in the world. This is primarily a process of elimination: once you have removed all the dead language, the second-hand dogma, the truths that are not your own but other people's, the mottos, the slogans, the out-and-out lies of your nation, the myths of your historical moment—once you have removed all that warps experience into a shape you do not recognize and do not believe in—what you are left with is something approximating the truth of your own conception."

—Zadie Smith

"A story isn't a charcoal sketch, where every stroke lies on the surface to be seen. It's an oil painting, filled with layers that the author must uncover so carefully to show its beauty."

—AMELIA ATWATER-RHODES

*"Read over your compositions,
and wherever you meet with a passage
which you think is particularly fine,
strike it out."*

—Samuel Johnson

"It takes a heap of loafing to write a book."

— GERTRUDE STEIN

"The purpose of a writer is to keep civilization from destroying itself."

—ALBERT CAMUS

"I hate writing, I love having written."

—DOROTHY PARKER

"People will tell you that writing is too difficult, that it's impossible to get your work published, that you might as well hang yourself. Meanwhile, they'll keep writing and you'll have hanged yourself."

—JOHN GARDNER

"I firmly believe every book was meant to be written."

— MARCHETTE CHUTE

"Find out the reason that commands you to write; see whether it has spread its roots into the very depth of your heart; confess to yourself you would have to die if you were forbidden to write."

— RAINER MARIA RILKE

"I start with a tingle, a kind of feeling of the story I will write. Then come the characters, and they take over, they make the story."

— KAREN BLIXEN

"Deliver me from writers who say the way they live doesn't matter. I'm not sure a bad person can write a good book. If art doesn't make us better, then what on earth is it for."

—ALICE WALKER

"It's so easy and quick to publish one's work in today's digital, instant gratification world, but that doesn't mean you should; not yet, anyway. Hone your writing skills first before you take that leap."

— CAROL HOENIG

"Perhaps I write for no one. Perhaps for the same person children are writing for when they scrawl their names in the snow."

— M A R G A R E T   A T W O O D

"When I write, I feel like an armless, legless man with a crayon in his mouth."

— KURT VONNEGUT

"When asked, 'How do you write?'
I invariably answer, 'One word at a time,'
and the answer is invariably dismissed.
But that is all it is. It sounds too simple
to be true, but consider the Great Wall
of China, if you will: one stone at a time,
man. That's all. One stone at a time. But
I've read you can see that motherfucker
from space without a telescope."

— STEPHEN KING

"With writing, we have second chances."

—J ONATHAN S AFRAN F OER

"*Perfectionism is the voice of the oppressor, the enemy of the people. It will keep you cramped and insane your whole life, and it is the main obstacle between you and a shitty first draft. I think perfectionism is based on the obsessive belief that if you run carefully enough, hitting each stepping-stone just right, you won't have to die. The truth is that you will die anyway and that a lot of people who aren't even looking at their feet are going to do a whole lot better than you, and have a lot more fun while they're doing it.*"

— ANNE LAMOTT

"I write to connect with my soul, to find out my true purpose in life, and that is when it comes—and comes strong—as if I have been writing these words forever. As if I have written them in other lifetimes. In the end, these words were mine even before I wrote them."

—CHRISTINA RASMUSSEN

"Writing is prayer."

— F R A N Z   K A F K A

"Writing is like a jigsaw puzzle with large chunks of pieces missing. Finding the missing pieces of your story is what makes or breaks the story. It is the content that either pleases readers and hooks them into moving to the next page or inspires them to use your book for kindling on a cold winter night. When a story comes together it just feels right."

— KARL ROBB

"Writing simply means no dependent clauses, no dangling things, no flashbacks, and keeping the subject near the predicate. . .Simple, short sentences don't always work. You have to do tricks with pacing, alternate long sentences with short, to keep it vital and alive . . . Virtually every page is a cliffhanger— you've got to force them to turn it."

— DR. SEUSS

"In order to write the book you want to write, in the end you have to become the person you need to become to write that book."

—Junot Diaz

"Writer's block is just a symptom of feeling like you have nothing to say, combined with the rather weird idea that you should feel the need to say something. Why? If you have something to say, then say it. If not, enjoy the silence while it lasts. The noise will return soon enough."

—HUGH MACLEOD

"A good poem is a contribution to reality. The world is never the same once a good poem has been added to it. A good poem helps to change the shape of the universe, helps to extend everyone's knowledge of himself and the world around him."

— DYLAN THOMAS

"Words can be like X-rays if you use them properly—they'll go through anything. You read and you're pierced."

—ALDOUS HUXLEY

"Mistakes and accidents,
or gifts of sheer inspiration, can enter
at any time to fertilize the process with
fresh information."

—STEPHEN NACHMANOVITCH

"My own experience is that once a story has been written, one has to cross out the beginning and the end. It is there that we authors do most of our lying."

—Anton Chekhov

"Any writer worth his salt writes to please himself... It's a self-exploratory operation that is endless. An exorcism of not necessarily his demon, but of his divine discontent."

— HARPER LEE

"The writer should never be ashamed of staring. There is nothing that does not require his attention."

— FLANNERY O'CONNOR

"Language is my whore, my mistress, my wife, my pen-friend, my checkout girl. Language is a complimentary moist lemon-scented cleansing square or handy freshen-up wipette. Language is the breath of God, the dew on a fresh apple, it's the soft rain of dust that falls into a shaft of morning sun when you pull from an old bookshelf a forgotten volume of erotic diaries…"

— STEPHEN FRY

"You can be an inept writer and dismal salesperson and hit the jackpot if your book strikes a nerve. But looking for a nerve-striking theme that will fly around the world, be made into a movie, and have publishers, readers, and Hollywood begging for sequels is counterproductive to good writing. The real beauty of being a writer is that you can work in bed."

— NANCY DEVILLE

"Writing is turning one's worst moments into money."

—J . P . D O N L E A V Y

"Every few weeks she would shut herself up in her room, put on her scribbling suit, and fall into a vortex, as she expressed it, writing away at her novel with all her heart and soul, for till that was finished she could find no peace."

— LOUISA MAY ALCOTT

"The author must keep his mouth shut when his work starts to speak."

— FRIEDRICH NIETZSCHE

"Sometimes a book isn't a heartbreaking work of staggering genius. Sometimes it's the only story you knew how to tell."

— TAHEREH MAFI

"I write to give myself strength. I write to be the characters that I am not. I write to explore all the things I'm afraid of."

—J OSS W HEDON

"There are three difficulties in authorship: to write anything worth publishing, to find honest men to publish it, and to get sensible men to read it."

— CHARLES CALEB COTTON

"It's better to write about things you feel than about things you know about."

—L. P. HARTLEY

"I think, to a poet, the human community is like the community of birds to a bird, singing to each other. Love is one of the reasons we are singing to one another, love of language itself, love of sound, love of singing itself, and love of the other birds."

—Sharon Olds

*"Writing is a form of therapy;
sometimes I wonder how all those who
do not write, compose, or paint can
manage to escape the madness,
melancholia, the panic and fear which
is inherent in a human situation."*

— GRAHAM GREENE

"The only thing worth writing about is people. People. Human beings. Men and women whose individuality must be created, line by line, insight by insight. If you do not do it, the story is a failure."

— HARLAN ELLISON

"I love writing. I love the swirl and swing of words as they tangle with human emotions."

—James A. Michener

"It has taken me years of struggle, hard work, and research to learn to make one simple gesture, and I know enough about the art of writing to realize that it would take as many years of concentrated effort to write one simple, beautiful sentence."

— Isadora Duncan

"All that I hope to say in books, all that I ever hope to say, is that I love the world."

—E.B. White

"I don't know where my ideas come from, but I know where they come to. They come to my desk, and if I'm not there, they go away again."

— PHILIP PULLMAN

143

"I just sit at my typewriter and curse a bit."

— P.G. WODEHOUSE

"I'm writing an unauthorized autobiography."

—STEVEN WRIGHT

"Don't you wish you had a job like mine? All you have to do is think up a certain number of words! Plus, you can repeat words! And they don't even have to be true!"

— DAVE BARRY

"The task of a writer consists in being able to make something out of an idea."

— THOMAS MANN

"You cannot depend on your eyes when your imagination is out of focus."

—Joan Didion

"If you want to be a writer,
you have to write every day. . . .You don't
go to a well once but daily. You don't skip
a child's breakfast or forget to wake up in
the morning."

—WALTER MOSLEY

"You don't make art out of good intentions."

— GUSTAVE FLAUBERT

"There was a moment when I changed from an amateur to a professional. I assumed the burden of a profession, which is to write even when you don't want to, don't much like what you're writing, and aren't writing particularly well."

— AGATHA CHRISTIE

"I don't wait for moods. You accomplish nothing is you do that. Your mind must know it has got to get down to work."

— PEARL S. BUCK

"In a good bookroom you feel in some mysterious way that you are absorbing the wisdom contained in all the books through your skin, without even opening them."

— M A R K T W A I N

"You should write because you love the shape of stories and sentences and the creation of different words on a page. Writing comes from reading, and reading is the finest teacher of how to write."

—E. ANNIE PROULX

"In writing, you must kill all your darlings."

— WILLIAM FAULKNER

"Concentrate on what you want to say to yourself and your friends. Follow your inner moonlight; don't hide the madness. You say what you want to say when you don't care who's listening."

—ALLEN GINSBERG

"If you are in difficulties with a book, try the element of surprise: attack it at an hour when it isn't expecting it."

— H . G . W E L L S

"I don't think writers are sacred,
but words are. They deserve respect.
If you get the right ones in the right
order, you might nudge the world a little
or make a poem that children will speak
for you when you are dead."

—Tom Stoppard

"A good book isn't written,

it's rewritten."

— PHYLLIS A. WHITNEY

"I don't teach writing. I teach patience. Toughness. Stubbornness. The willingness to fail. I teach the life. The odd thing is most of the things that stop an inexperienced writer are so far from the truth as to be nearly beside the point. When you feel global doubt about your talent, that is your talent. People who have no talent don't have any doubt."

— R I C H A R D   B A U S C H

"If you really want to be a writer, nobody can stop you—and if you don't, nobody can help you."

—ALMA ALEXANDER

"For me writing is a constant surrender to flow. Some days I'm too stubborn to let go. Other days I get caught in the current of other things. Yet, when my wave from the tide does come in, and I dive into the sea of inspiration, I feel my inner-guide take the lead, and I sail through the 'world of words' with ease. Then when I come back to my body and to the room, I look back on what was written, and I smile. 'Wow. You are amazing!' I tell my Higher Self, as I remain in a state of wonderment."

— MICHELLE SKALETSKI-BOYD

"Writing is a delicious agony."

— GWENDOLYN BROOKS

"Writing a novel is a terrible experience, during which the hair often falls out and the teeth decay. I'm always irritated by people who imply that writing fiction is an escape from reality. It is a plunge into reality and it's very shocking to the system."

— FLANNERY O'CONNOR

"Do you think that Hemingway knew he was a writer at twenty years old? No, he did not. Or Fitzgerald, or Wolfe. This is a difficult concept to grasp. Hemingway didn't know he was Ernest Hemingway when he was a young man. Faulkner didn't know he was William Faulkner. But they had to take the first step. They had to call themselves writers. That is the first revolutionary act a writer has to make. It takes courage. But it's necessary."

—PAT CONROY

"I must write it all out, at any cost. Writing is thinking. It is more than living, for it is being conscious of living."

—ANNE MORROW LINDBERGH

"When I stop working the rest of the day is posthumous. I'm only really alive when I'm writing."

— TENNESSEE WILLIAMS

"Let us record the atoms as they fall upon the mind in the order in which they fall, let us trace the pattern, however disconnected and incoherent in appearance, which each sight or incident scores upon the consciousness. Let us not take it for granted that life exists more fully in what is commonly thought big than in what is commonly thought small."

— VIRGINIA WOOLF

"I got two years into the novel and got completely stymied and felt like it was an utter flop. I wanted to put it aside but my wife talked me out of it. She said she cared too much about these characters and wanted to find out what became of them. I had to start all over again, keeping the characters but reinventing the story completely and leaving behind almost every element with the exception of the birth that goes wrong—that was the only significant element that I preserved."

— MICHAEL CHABON

"Whenever I am lost, I pick up a pen. Even if my writing in that moment is bad, it's okay because it is home. No matter how confused, sad, uncreative, scared, stressed, or tired I feel, home is where I want to be and I get there through writing."

— MELANI WARD

"For it would seem—her case proved it—that we write, not with the fingers, but with the whole person. The nerve which controls the pen winds itself about every fiber of our being, threads the heart, pierces the liver."

—V IRGINIA W OOLF

"It is the imagination that gives shape to the universe."

— B A R R Y   L O P E Z

"Originality has nothing to do with priority. An image is like a musical key; just because someone used G-minor before doesn't make Mozart a copycat."

— STEPHEN MITCHELL

"For it would seem—her case proved it—that we write, not with the fingers, but with the whole person. The nerve which controls the pen winds itself about every fiber of our being, threads the heart, pierces the liver."

—VIRGINIA WOOLF

"Some things are hard to write about.
After something happens to you,
you go to write it down, and either
you over dramatize it, or underplay it,
exaggerate the wrong parts or ignore the
important ones. At any rate, you never
write it quite the way you want to."

— Sylvia Plath

"Exercise the writing muscle every day, even if it is only a letter, notes, a title list, a character sketch, a journal entry. Writers are like dancers, like athletes. Without that exercise, the muscles seize up."

—JANE YOLEN

"At times I believed that the last page of my book and the last page of my life were one and the same, that when my book ended I'd end, a great wind would sweep through my rooms carrying the pages away, and when the air cleared of all those fluttering white sheets the room would be silent, the chair where I sat empty."

—NICOLE KRAUSS

"Almost anyone can be an author;
the business is to collect money and fame
from this state of being."

— A. A. MILNE

"Writing is thinking on paper."

—William Zinsser

"Writing gives you a voice that allows you to share your unique story and vision with the world."

— PAUL NOVELLO

"The easiest way to do art is to dispense with success and failure altogether and just get on with it."

— Stephen Nachmanovitch

"Yes, creation is moving toward us;

life is moving toward us all the time.

We back away, but it keeps pushing

toward us."

—J O A N   H A L I F A X

"Especially as artists, we have to celebrate our memories."

— MEINRAD CRAIGHEAD

"Writing daily in my journal was the life raft that kept me afloat after I turned eleven. Inside its sturdy covers lived all my hopes, dreams, fears, successes, and failures. For years I scribbled page after page, book upon book, in handwriting now illegible to me. For the first time in my life I was heard and loved unconditionally, carried home by a seaworthy craft."

— RENEE BARIBEAU

"Be ruthless about protecting writing days, i.e., do not cave in to endless requests to have 'essential' and 'long overdue' meetings on those days. Some people do not seem to grasp that I still have to sit down in peace and write the books, apparently believing that they pop up like mushrooms without my connivance."

— J . K .   R O W L I N G

"As you begin to pay attention to your own stories and what they say about you, you will enter the exciting process of becoming, as you should be, the author of your own life, the creator of your own possibilities."

—MANDY AFTEL

"One writes to make a home for one's self, in time, in others' minds."

—Alfred Kazin

"Finally, one just has to shut up, sit down, and write."

—NATALIE GOLDBERG

"When I run into writer's block, I find it helpful to imagine how the subject matter applies to my life. I then write about my own epiphanies or experiences from applying the principles that I intend to teach. If I get nervous, I try to imagine the whole world reading my book . . . naked!"

— WILL HARRIS

*"Learn to trust your own judgment,
learn inner independence, learn to trust
that time will sort good from bad—
including your own bad."*

— DORIS LESSING

"Great writing can be conjured from great injustice."

— LANCE MORROW

*"Every word a woman writes
changes the story of the world,
revises the official version."*

— CAROLYN SEE

"Art is not just ornamental, an enhancement of life, but a path in itself, a way out of the predictable and conventional, a map to self-discovery."

— GABRIELLE ROTH

"Writing is the only thing that when I do it, I don't feel I should be doing something else."

—GLORIA STEINEM

"A creative writer can do his best only with what lies within the range and character of his deepest sympathies."

— WILLA CATHER

"An essential portion of any artist's labor is not creation so much as invocation."

— LEWIS HYDE

"You have to write the book that wants to be written. And if the book will be too difficult for grownups, then you write it for children."

— MADELEINE L'ENGLE

*"In a general sense, all artists
are shamans, insomuch as they are
channeling images or concepts on behalf
of the collective."*

—VICKI NOBLE

"Unless a capacity to dream and fantasize is there, derivative things will be made."

—PETER LONDON

"Our creativity does not consist in being right all the time, but in making of all our experiences, including the apparently mistaken and imperfect ones, a holy whole."

— MATTHEW FOX

"First thoughts have tremendous energy. It is the way the mind first flashes on something."

—Natalie Goldberg

"The truth dazzles gradually, or else the whole world would be blind."

— EMILY DICKINSON

"In a dark time, the eye begins to see."

—THEODORE ROETHKE

"Art is a personal gift that changes the recipient."

—SETH GODIN

"It is the function of art to renew our perception. What we are familiar with we cease to see."

—A N A Ï S   N I N

"Predictability is the death of creativity for a writer."

—Stephanie Gunning

"The way to get started is to quit talking and begin doing."

—WALT DISNEY

"The writer must write what he has to say, not speak it."

—ERNEST HEMINGWAY

"Wit has truth in it; wisecracking is simply calisthenics with words."

— D O R O T H Y P A R K E R

"Fantasy is hardly an escape from reality. It's a way of understanding it."

— LLOYD ALEXANDER

"Everything in life is writable about if you have the outgoing guts to do it, and the imagination to improvise. The worst enemy to creativity is self-doubt."

—SYLVIA PLATH

"After nourishment, shelter, and companionship, stories are the thing we need most in the world."

— PHILIP PULLMAN

*"Don't tell me the moon is shining;
show me the glint of light on
broken glass."*

—A N T O N   C H E K H O V

"We have to continually be jumping off cliffs and developing our wings on the way down."

— KURT VONNEGUT

"The scariest moment is always just before you start."

— STEPHEN KING

"This is how you do it: You sit down at the keyboard and you put one word after another until it's done. It's that easy, and that hard."

—NEIL GAIMAN

"I think writing is, by definition,
an optimistic act."

— MICHAEL CUNNINGHAM

"Writing is a performance, like singing an aria or dancing a jig."

—STEPHEN GREENBLATT

"The less conscious one is of being 'a writer,' the better the writing."

— PICO IYER

"Writing is a socially acceptable form of schizophrenia."

— E.L. DOCTOROW

"Writing transports one's inspiration from the heart to humanity."

—ALLISON MASLAN

"Imagery comes directly out of your own core. The more precise the attention you pay to the world around you, the more you will rejoice in, the more stuff will be in you that rises as real metaphor and simile, expressive, precise, powerful, felt. Anything we truly experience and take in is the stuff of metaphor."

— MARGE PIERCY

"Write something to suit yourself and many people will like it; write something to suit everybody and scarcely anyone will care for it."

—JESSE STUART

"All you have to do is write one true sentence. Write the truest sentence that you know."

—Ernest Hemingway

"The role of a writer is not to say what we can all say, but what we are unable to say."

—A N A ï S   N I N

"Writing a book is a horrible, exhausting struggle, like a long bout with some painful illness. One would never undertake such a thing if one were not driven on by some demon whom one can neither resist nor understand."

—George Orwell

"Nothing's a better cure for writer's block than to eat ice cream right out of the carton."

— D o n   R o f f

"We can destroy what we have written,

but we cannot unwrite it."

—A N T H O N Y   B U R G E S S

"I'm writing a book. I've got the page numbers done."

— STEVEN WRIGHT

"In good writing, words become one with things."

— RALPH WALDO EMERSON

"*The writer who cares more about words than about story—characters, action, setting, atmosphere—is unlikely to create a vivid and continuous dream; he gets in his own way too much; in his poetic drunkenness, he can't tell the cart—and its cargo—from the horse.*"

—JOHN GARDNER

"There is no agony like bearing an untold story inside you."

— Z O R A   N E A L E   H U R S T O N

"I think the first duty of all art, including fiction of any kind, is to entertain. That is to say, to hold interest. No matter how worthy the message of something, if it's dull, you're just not communicating."

—POUL ANDERSON

"Those who write clearly have readers. Those who write obscurely have commentators."

—ALBERT CAMUS

"Writing gives you the illusion of control, and then you realize it's just an illusion, that people are going to bring their own stuff into it."

— DAVID SEDARIS

"Asking a working writer what he thinks about critics is like asking a lamppost what he thinks about dogs."

— CHRISTOPHER HAMPTON

"This manuscript of yours that has just come back from another editor is a precious package. Don't consider it rejected. Consider that you've addressed it 'to the editor who can appreciate my work' and it has simply come back stamped 'Not at this address.' Just keep looking for the right address."

— BARBARA KINGSOLVER

"I write for the same reason I breathe—

because if I didn't, I would die."

—ISAAC ASIMOV

"Books aren't written, they're rewritten. Including your own. It is one of the hardest things to accept, especially after the seventh rewrite hasn't quite done it."

—MICHAEL CRICHTON

"The most valuable of all talents is that of never using two words when one will do."

— Thomas Jefferson

"A writer should have another lifetime to see if he's appreciated."

—JORGE LUIS BORGES

"There are many reasons why novelists write—but they all have one thing in common: a need to create an alternative world."

—John Fowles

"Forget all the rules. Forget about being published. Write for yourself and celebrate writing."

— MELINDA HAYNES

"Close the door. Write with no one looking over your shoulder. Don't try to figure out what other people want to hear from you; figure out what you have to say. It's the one and only thing you have to offer."

—BARBARA KINGSOLVER

"Writing is the best way to talk without being interrupted."

—Jules Renard

*"I learned that you should feel
when writing, not like Lord Byron on
a mountaintop, but like a child stringing
beads in kindergarten—happy,
absorbed and quietly putting one bead
on after another."*

— B R E N D A   U E L A N D

"If you ask me what I came to do in this world, I, an artist, will answer you: I am here to live out loud."

— EMILE ZOLA

"A blank piece of paper is God's way of telling us how hard it to be God."

—SIDNEY SHELDON

"Writing is not necessarily something to be ashamed of, but do it in private and wash your hands afterwards."

— R OBERT A. H EINLEIN

"I write to discover what I know."

—FLANNERY O'CONNOR

"There is nothing to writing. All you do is sit down at a typewriter and bleed."

— ERNEST HEMINGWAY

"If writing seems hard, it's because it is hard. It's one of the hardest things people do."

—WILLIAM ZINSSER

"There's no such thing as writer's block. That was invented by people in California who couldn't write."

— Terry Pratchett

"The faster I write the better my output. If I'm going slow, I'm in trouble. It means I'm pushing the words instead of being pulled by them."

— R A Y M O N D   C H A N D L E R

"Writing a novel is like driving a car at night. You can only see as far as your headlights, but you can make the whole trip that way."

—E. L. DOCTOROW

"To be a writer is to sit down at one's desk in the chill portion of every day, and to write; not waiting for the little jet of the blue flame of genius to start from the breastbone—just plain going at it, in pain and delight. To be a writer is to throw away a great deal, not to be satisfied, to type again, and then again, and once more, and over and over."

—J OHN H ERSEY

"A writer never has a vacation. For a writer life consists of either writing or thinking about writing."

—Eugene Ionesco

"When once the itch of literature comes over a man, nothing can cure it but the scratching of a pen."

— SAMUEL LOVER

"Writing is its own reward."

— HENRY MILLER

"I love being a writer. What I can't stand is the paperwork."

— PETER DE VRIES

"How can one not dream while writing? It is the pen which dreams. The blank page gives the right to dream."

— GASTON BACHELARD

"People without hope not only don't write novels, but what is more to the point, they don't read them."

— FLANNERY O'CONNOR

"I write entirely to find out what I'm thinking, what I'm looking at, what I see and what it means. What I want and what I fear."

—JOAN DIDION

"If any man wish to write in a clear style, let him be first clear in his thoughts; and if any would write in a noble style, let him first possess a noble soul."

—JOHANN WOLFGANG VON GOETHE

"A writer is someone for whom writing is more difficult than it is for other people."

—Thomas Mann

"The brain that doesn't feed itself,

eats itself."

— G O R E V I D A L

"One of the things that draws writers to writing is that they can get things right that they got wrong in real life by writing about them."

—Tobias Wolff

"The ideal view for daily writing, hour for hour, is the blank brick wall of a cold-storage warehouse. Failing this, a stretch of sky will do, cloudless if possible."

— EDNA FERBER

"One of the really bad things you can do to your writing is to dress up the vocabulary, looking for long words because you're maybe a little bit ashamed of your short ones."

—STEPHEN KING

"My most important piece of advice to all you would-be writers: When you write, try to leave out all the parts readers skip."

— ELMORE LEONARD

"To produce a mighty book, you must choose a mighty theme."

— HERMAN MELVILLE

"Resist the temptation to try to use dazzling style to conceal weakness of substance."

— STANLEY SCHMIDT

"Books are never finished, they are merely abandoned."

—OSCAR WILDE

"The writer's only responsibility is to his art. He will be completely ruthless if he is a good one. . . . If a writer has to rob his mother, he will not hesitate; the Ode on a Grecian Urn is worth any number of old ladies."

—WILLIAM FAULKNER

"You can't wait for inspiration. You have to go after it with a club."

—JACK LONDON

"Amateurs sit and wait for inspiration,
the rest of us just get up and go to work."

— STEPHEN KING

Recommended Resources

Please visit www.StephanieGunning.com for more information on online home-study courses, workshops, books, and audio programs on professional book publishing. You'll find a variety of products and services there that are designed to support accomplished and first-time authors.

Free Newsletter
To subscribe to Stephanie Gunning's weekly online newsletter, "Get a Book Deal™ News," and be notified about trends in publishing, upcoming courses, webinars, live events, services, and product releases, go to www.StephanieGunning.com.

Editorial and Consulting Services
If you require editorial services, please send an email to contact@stephaniegunning.com briefly describing the nature of your project. A member of our staff will contact you in reply.

Get a Book Deal® Coaching

Being mentored in writing a book proposal or in preparing a strategic book-marketing platform and production plan for a self-published book is the quickest way to get the job done and ensure a successful outcome. Visit www.getaBookDealCoaching.com to get more details about our coaching programs. Space is limited, and therefore enrollment is by application.

Online Home-study Courses

Visit the "Services" page at www.StephanieGunning.com to find out about Stephanie's different training programs. Some are periodically offered live and others are recorded. Stephanie is the creator of "The Book Proposal Intensive," "Twitter for Authors," and "Book Marketing Training for Self-published Authors," among other courses.

Alphabetical Listing of Writers

About Stephanie Gunning

Stephanie Gunning is an internationally acclaimed mind-body-spirit writer, editor, and strategist whose work has contributed to the success in publishing of many of the most popular and well-recognized spiritual and personal growth thought leaders of our era, among them several *New York Times* bestselling authors. As a consultant, editor, and writer, her clients have included major publishing firms, top-caliber literary agencies, and innovative self-publishers. She has mastered the art of transforming powerful ideas into highly marketable books.

In addition to coauthoring and ghostwriting dozens of books, Stephanie leads creativity workshops, hosts webinars and gives lectures on publishing opportunities and skills, and is the creator of several online home-study courses and audio programs for writers. She is cofounder of Lincoln Square Books, a New York-based project management firm serving the editorial, production, and marketing needs of authors who independently publish.

17376753R00157

Made in the USA
Charleston, SC
08 February 2013